Violin

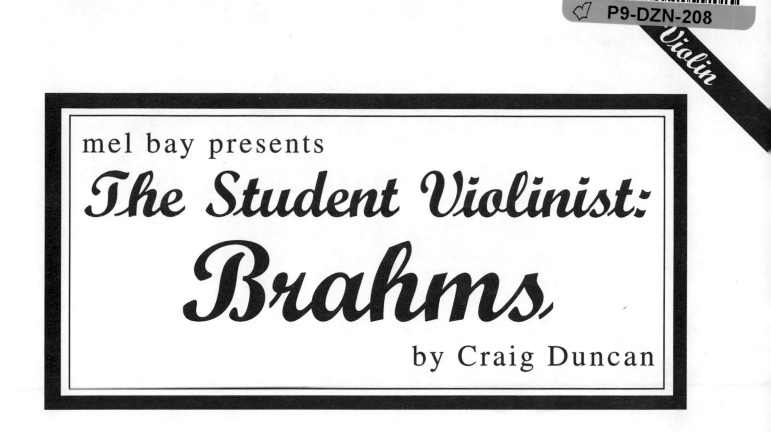

mel bay presents

The Student Violinist:
Brahms

by Craig Duncan

© 1997 BY MEL BAY PUBLICATIONS, INC., PACIFIC, MO 63069.
ALL RIGHTS RESERVED. INTERNATIONAL COPYRIGHT SECURED. B.M.I. MADE AND PRINTED IN U.S.A.

Visit us on the Web at http://www.melbay.com — E-mail us at email@melbay.com

Contents

This collection is taken from Brahms' incidental works, including his vocal pieces, songs, symphony themes and piano compositions. All of the pieces are playable in first position. The book begins with the easiest arrangements and progresses in level of difficulty. Most of the piano parts double the violin to aid in performance.

Lullaby

Johannes Brahms

Folk Song

Johannes Brahms

Andante

p dolce

ritard

Sonntag

Johannes Brahms

Waltz
Opus 39 Number 2

Johannes Brahms

Two German Folksongs

Johannes Brahms

Theme from Symphony No. 1

Opus 68 Fourth Movement

Johannes Brahms

Allegro non troppo

Waltz
Opus 39 Number 1

Johannes Brahms

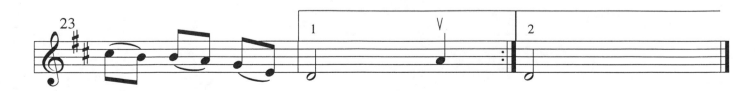

German Song

Johannes Brahms

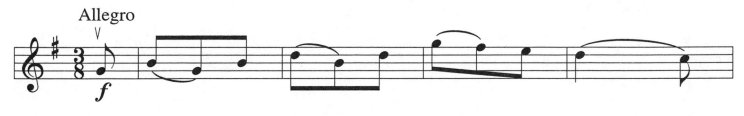

Intermezzo in A
Opus 118 Number 2

Johannes Brahms

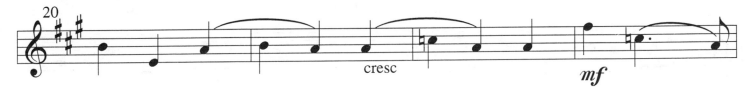

Anklänge

Johannes Brahms

Intermezzo
Opus 117 Number 1

Johannes Brahms

Romanze
Opus 118 Number 5

Johannes Brahms

mel bay presents

The Student Violinist: Brahms

by Craig Duncan

Visit us on the Web at http://www.melbay.com — E-mail us at email@melbay.com

Contents

This collection is taken from Brahms' incidental works, including his vocal pieces, songs, symphony themes and piano compositions. All of the pieces are playable in first position. The book begins with the easiest arrangements and progresses in level of difficulty. Most of the piano parts double the violin to aid in performance.

Lullaby

Johannes Brahms

Folk Song

Johannes Brahms

Violin

Piano

Sonntag

Johannes Brahms

Waltz
Opus 39 Number 2

Johannes Brahms

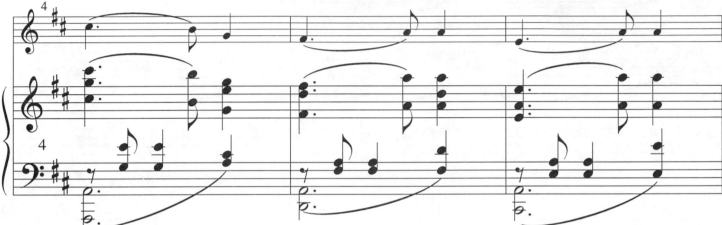

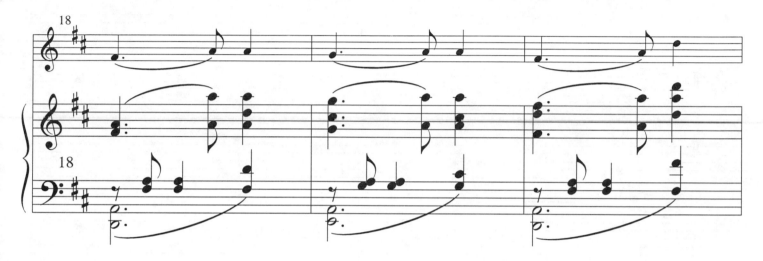

Two German Folksongs

Johannes Brahms

D.C. al Fine

Theme from Symphony No. 1

Opus 68 Fourth Movement

Johannes Brahms

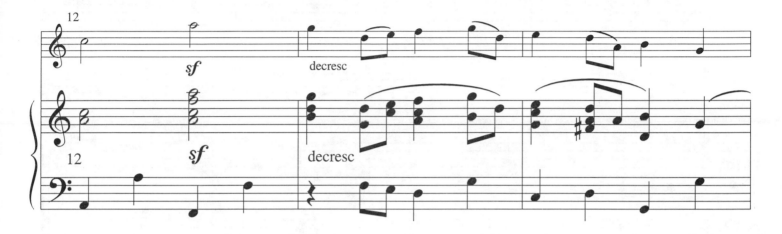

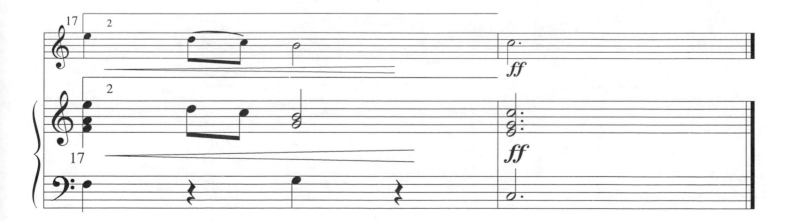

Waltz
Opus 39 Number 1

Johannes Brahms

Violin

Piano

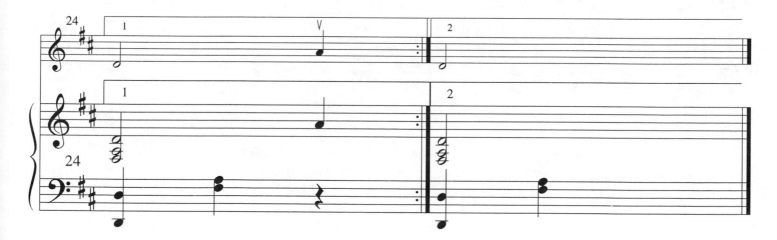

17

German Song

Johannes Brahms

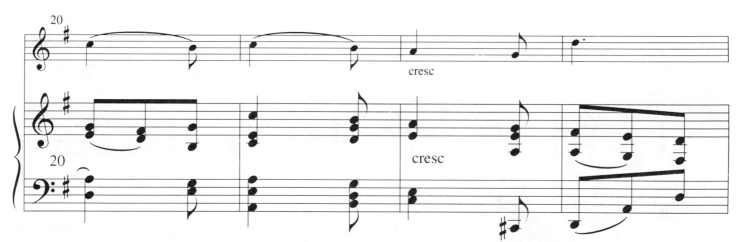

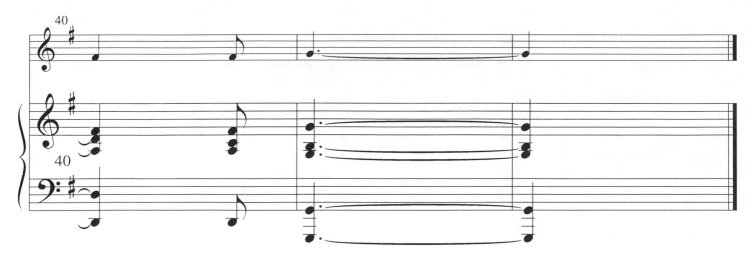

Intermezzo in A

Opus 118 Number 2

Johannes Brahms

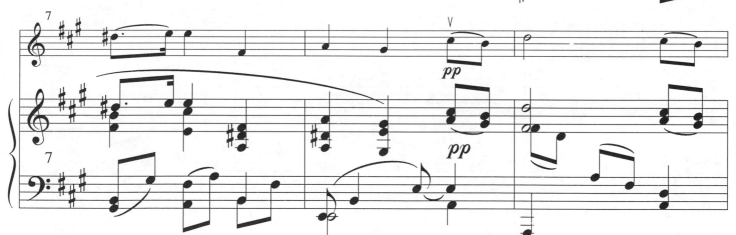

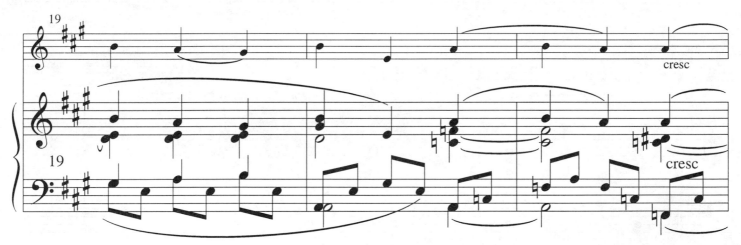

Anklänge

Johannes Brahms

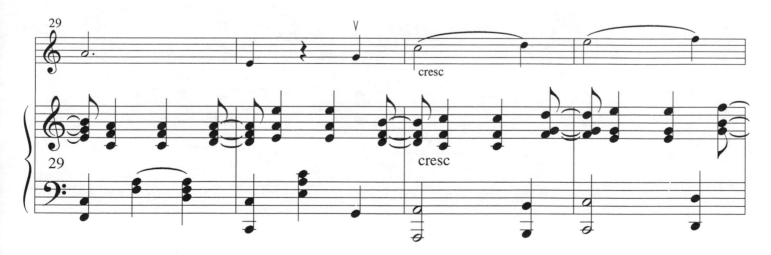

Intermezzo
Opus 117 Number 1

Johannes Brahms

Romanze
Opus 118 Number 5

Johannes Brahms